Life of the Honeybee

by Heiderose and Andreas Fischer-Nagel

A Carolrhoda Nature Watch Book

Carolrhoda Books, Inc./Minneapolis

Thanks to Dr. Basil Furgala, Department of Entomology, University of Minnesota, and Jerry Heaps, Registered Professional Entomologist, for their assistance with this book

Photograph on page 45 courtesy of Dr. Basil Furgala, University of Minnesota

This edition first published 1986 by Carolrhoda Books, Inc.
Original edition published 1983 by Kinderbuchverlag KBV Luzern AG,
Lucerne, Switzerland, under the title IM BIENENSTOCK © 1982
Translated from the German by Elise H. Scherer
Adapted by Carolrhoda Books, Inc.

Manufactured in the United States of America

This book is available in two editions:
Library binding by Carolrhoda Books, Inc.
Soft cover by First Avenue Editions
c/o The Lerner Group
241 First Avenue North
Minneapolis, MN 55401

LIBRARY OF CONGRESS CATALOGING-IN-PUBLICATION DATA

Fischer-Nagel, Heiderose.
  Life of the honeybee.

  Translation of: Im Bienenstock.
  "A Carolrhoda nature watch book."
  Includes index.
  Summary: Text and photographs present aspects of
the honeybee's life.
  1. Honeybee—Juvenile literature. [1. Honeybee.
2. Bees] I. Fischer-Nagel, Andreas. II. Title.
QL568.A6F5213 1986   595.79'9   85-13960
ISBN 0-87614-241-2 (lib. bdg.)
ISBN 0-87614-470-9 (pbk.)

6 7 8 9 10 11 – P/JR – 00 99 98 97 96 95

We've all seen honeybees busily flying from flower to flower on warm spring and summer days. Although they are common, honeybees are a rather misunderstood insect. Very few people really appreciate them for the helpful and fascinating creatures they are.

Honeybees belong to the scientific order *Hymenoptera.* This term comes from Greek words meaning "membrane wing" and describes the bees' thin, transparent wings. Of the many **species,** or kinds, of bees, honeybees are of the species *Apis mellifera.* The Latin *Apis* means "bee," and *mellifera* means "honey-bearer."

Honeybees are very helpful to humans. As their name suggests, they produce the sweet, delicious honey we enjoy as food. They also produce **beeswax,** which is used to make candles, lipsticks, lotions, and many other useful items. One of the honeybee's most important jobs is to **pollinate** flowers so that they will produce seeds and fruit. In this book, we will learn more about how honeybees perform their important duties.

Honeybees live in colonies in hives. There are many wild honeybee colonies that make their homes in hollow trees. But most honeybees today are raised and cared for by **beekeepers.** In earlier times beekeepers used handwoven baskets, or **skeps,** as beehives. Today most

beehives are wooden boxes. This photo shows some hives in a field in Germany. Hives in North America look slightly different.

Each beehive contains many individual honeycombs with hexagonal (six-sided) cells made of beeswax. The honeycombs are used for storing nectar, honey, and pollen from flowers and for raising young bees. In the photo above you can see a honeycomb up close.

Honeybees live in a well-ordered colony that may contain from 35 to 50 thousand members. Three kinds of individuals live in the honeybee society: one **queen** (fertile female), thousands of **workers** (infertile females), and hundreds of **drones,** or male bees.

The body of the honeybee is divided into three parts. The **head** includes the eyes, the antennae, and the chewing and sucking mouth parts with a long tongue. Four wings and six legs grow on the **thorax.** The third part is the **abdomen.** At the end of the abdomen is the bee's stinger.

The drone (above left) is larger than the worker and has very large eyes. Drones can also be identified by their rounded abdomens. Workers have pointed abdomens.

The worker bees (above right) are the most industrious honeybees in the colony. Workers live only six weeks during the summer season. In this short time, they can accomplish many different duties in the hive. They build the honeycomb, and they feed the grow-ing bees that hatch from eggs laid by the queen. They clean the hive, and they fly out to collect food and water. Worker bees also defend the colony from creatures that may want to steal honey from the hive.

The drones do not work at all. Their only task is to mate with the queen. The drones that successfully mate with the queen die shortly thereafter. The rest of the drones die soon, too, since they cannot help the workers take care of the hive.

The queen is cared for by the workers in the colony. She is surrounded by a "court" that forms itself around her wherever she stops. The bees in this court always face the queen and constantly feed and groom her.

The queen pictured on the following page is longer and slimmer than both the worker bees and the drones. She has been marked by a beekeeper with a spot whose color and number give details about the queen such as when she was born. Queens can live for up to five years, but in a beekeeper's hive they are usually replaced each year.

The queen's only function in the hive is to lay eggs, making her solely responsible for providing the next generation of bees. Before a queen can lay eggs, she must mate with one or more drones on a "mating flight." The drone's **sperm,** or reproductive cells, are carried in the queen's body throughout her life and remain there ready for each time she lays eggs.

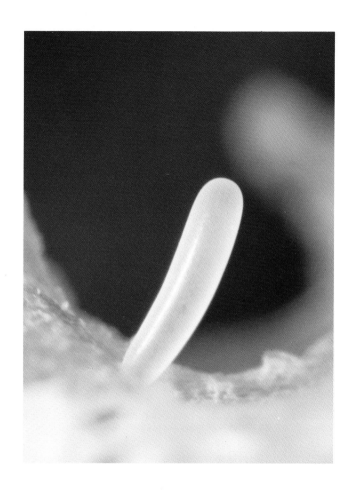

Queens lay up to 1,500 eggs a day, one at a time, each in one of the cells of the honeycomb. According to the size of the cell, the queen decides whether to put in a fertilized egg, out of which a worker will emerge, or an unfertilized egg, which will become a drone. Drone eggs are laid in somewhat larger cells than those for worker eggs.

Before laying an egg, the queen checks the cell to see if it is clean and how big it is. Then she inserts her abdomen and pushes out an oblong egg, about the size of the head of a pin, which sticks to the bottom of the cell. Cells that contain eggs and young growing bees are called **brood cells.**

Three days after the egg is laid, the first stage of the bee's development is complete. A small **larva** hatches from the egg, looking like a little white worm. This is the second stage of the bee's life cycle. The larva grows at an amazing rate. In six days its size has increased 500 times. It is fed by worker bees, who secrete **royal jelly,** a protein-rich substance, from special glands. Then, after the first three days, the larva receives only a pollen-and-honey mixture called bee bread. (Queen bees, how-

ever, are fed royal jelly throughout their development.) Nine days after the egg is laid, the worker bees cap the larva's cell with wax produced in special wax glands.

After the cell is capped, a period of rest begins during which the larva changes into a **pupa,** the third stage in the bee's development. It spins a silky cocoon around itself and lies in its cell while many changes take place in its body.

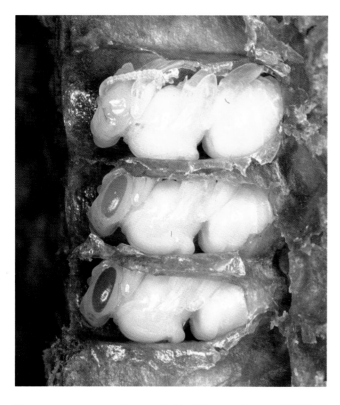

A glimpse into capped cells shows that the growing bees lie on their backs during the pupa stage (above left). Their bodies are completely white; at this point only the eyes are visible. In the middle of the pupa's head (below left) you can distinguish three tiny specks. These are the bee's three **simple eyes,** or **ocelli,** which can perceive darkness and light. The bee's large, sensitive **compound eyes** are the eyes with which it actually sees.

Twenty-one days after the egg was laid, the full-grown adult worker bee emerges. It eats away the wax cap of its cell, slips out, and immediately begins its "busy-as-a-bee" life. The drone needs somewhat longer for its development—24 days—and the queen needs just 16 days.

In the picture above, all stages of development are arranged in a circle: from the tiny egg at the top through the larvae and pupae in different stages of growth to the young bee in the middle. The cycle of change in the bee's growth—from egg to larva to pupa to adult—is called **complete metamorphosis.** Ants, beetles, butterflies, and moths are examples of other insects that undergo complete metamorphosis.

After emerging from their cells, worker bees usually spend the first three weeks of their lives in the hive. Because of this they are sometimes called **house bees** during this time. For about the first five days, house bees are responsible for "housecleaning" duties. They clean out brood cells to make them ready for new eggs. They also remove honeybees that have died in the hive and remove the dead bodies of other insects that may have invaded the hive.

For the next seven days, young workers serve as **nurse bees,** feeding larvae on royal jelly.

One of the most important jobs in the beehive is the building of the honeycomb. Worker bees perform this task from the 13th to the 16th day of their lives. Thousands of new cells can be constructed daily by the builder bees. To do this, they use wax that they secrete out of the wax glands in their abdomens. The wax is secreted as a liquid that quickly hardens into small plate-like drops or scales, as you see in the photo above left. The workers pass the wax scales to their mouths and knead them into small, soft lumps with their jaws, or **mandibles.** Out of many, many little balls of beeswax a honeycomb, with hundreds of six-sided cells, is formed.

Workers sometimes "hang" together in a chain, all the while producing wax through their wax glands.

From day 16 to day 20, workers may become **guard bees.** Here you see the entrance to a beehive. What a commotion there is! Actually, activity in the hive proceeds very smoothly. The guard bees help maintain this order. Because each beehive member carries the same scent, each new arrival is checked by the guard bees. That way they make sure no intruders enter the beehive.

Some guard bees sit at the hive entrance and stretch their backs up high, exposing their scent-releasing glands. With their wings, they fan the scent of the hive toward the arriving bees, making their return home easier.

Guard bees are ready for action at the slightest disturbance. Often, other honeybees, insects, or even a mouse may try to come into the hive in search of honey. Any creature that tries to invade the hive is in big trouble! The guard bees attack the enemy, as can be seen in the photo on the right, in which the honeybees are attacking a wasp. With their excellent attack skills they can defeat not only the wasp but also the bigger and stronger hornet.

Both the wasp (above left) and the hornet (below left) are black and yellow. The hornet is bigger, however, and its thorax is brown and not black in color like the wasp's. Although the hornet's stinger is larger than the wasp's, it is not more dangerous. The assumption that three hornet stings could kill a person was proved wrong long ago.

Worker honeybees have painful stings, too. The picture above shows an enlarged bee stinger with a drop of **venom** on it. A bee will sting only if she believes herself or the hive to be in danger. Because it has tiny barbs like those on a fish hook, the stinger tears off and is left behind in the victim's flesh when the honeybee flies away. The stinging apparatus remains "alive" and bores deeper and deeper into the flesh by reflex movements. This causes the venom to be pumped into the wound. Because a part of its body remains in the victim's flesh, a honeybee dies shortly after stinging a person or animal.

Drones have no stingers at all. Queen bees usually only sting other queens. Because they have smooth, curved stingers that are easily pulled out from the victim's body, queens do not lose their stingers and do not die after stinging.

During the last three weeks of their lives, workers fly out of the hive as **forager**, or **field**, bees to fulfill their new task: carrying pollen and nectar from flowers to the beehive. They collect their loads of pollen and nectar, and then return to the hive to deposit them into cells.

During a foraging trip, an individual bee will collect pollen from just one kind of plant, often returning to the same kind for many days. By collecting pollen from just one kind of plant, each bee helps with the **pollination** of the blossoms. When the worker crawls around on the blossom, the pollen, containing male reproductive cells, clings to the fine hairs of her body. The pollen is then carried from one blossom to another of the same kind, where it sticks to the female parts of that flower. Only after pollination can **fertilization**, or the union of male and female cells, take place. Without fertilization, plants would not produce fruit or seeds. Without seeds, no new plants could grow.

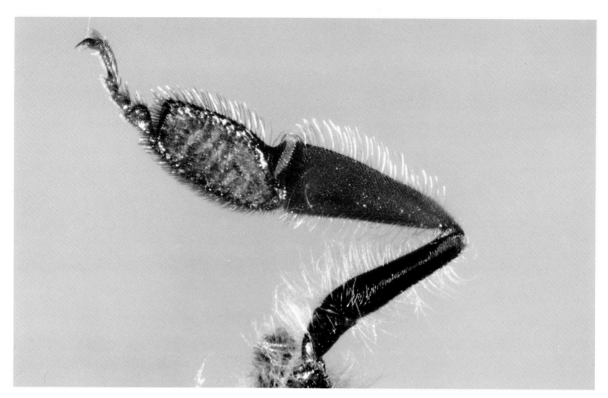

Pollen is carried in small **pollen baskets** on the outer sides of the worker's hind legs (above left). In the picture below left you can see pollen baskets filled with countless grains of pollen. In order to fill the baskets with pollen, the bee uses small brushes on the hind legs, which can easily be seen in the pictures. With her mouth parts the honeybee scrapes the pollen from the blossoms and with brushes on her legs secures it in the pollen baskets. The pollen is then taken back to the hive and stored as food for the honeybees.

The picture above shows a worker bee that has just returned with a heavy load of pollen collected during a foraging flight.

In addition to pollen, honeybees collect nectar, the sugary juice found in flowers. A worker sucks the sweet nectar with her straw-like tongue and stores it in her **crop,** or **honey stomach,** a special sac separate from the regular stomach. Sometimes honeybees must crawl quite deep into a blossom in order to reach the nectar. Because of this it is almost impossible for a honeybee to leave the flower without also being covered by pollen.

In the large picture you see a honeybee that has just landed on a harebell blossom. In the picture on the right, the blossom has been cut away so that you can watch the honeybee at work. You can see exactly how she clutches the inner parts of the blossom with her legs and sucks the nectar with her long tongue.

When the honeybee has collected as much as she can carry, she flies back to her hive. There she **regurgitates** the nectar and spreads it in a cell or gives it to other worker bees. In passing the nectar back and forth between bees, important enzymes are added to it. The enzymes, along with the evaporation of water that occurs in the 95° F (35° C) hive, turns the nectar into honey. The honey is stored in cells.

In this photo, filled honey cells can be seen glistening in the light. The cells that appear yellow are filled with pollen. The honey serves the bees as food, and they must save enough to last them the winter. To prevent the honey from draining out of the comb, each cell slants upward a little. Only if a honeycomb is turned over, as in the picture above left, can the honey run out. The beekeeper checks regularly to see if the honeycombs are full. Some beekeepers wear protective clothing to keep them safe from an angry bee's sting.

Honeybees have an uncanny ability to find blossoms that are especially rich in nectar and pollen. Worker bees communicate information about good food "finds" with an amazing "sign language." When worker field bees find an abundant supply of food, they return to the hive and perform a special dance on the face of the comb that shows the other workers where to find the food. While they dance, they also provide information about the kinds of flowers they've found by bringing back with them the scent of the blossoms.

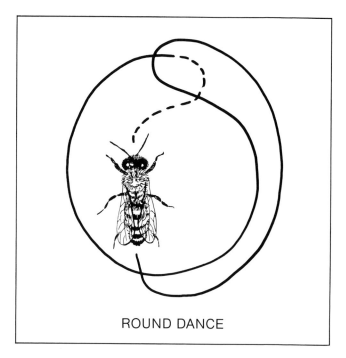

ROUND DANCE

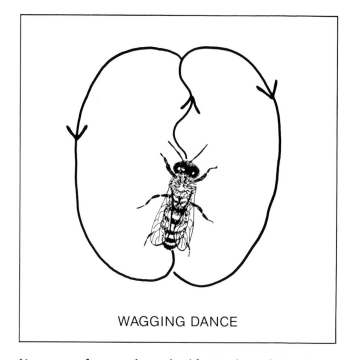

WAGGING DANCE

There are two kinds of dances. The **round dance** is performed when the food is close to the hive—about 100 yards or less. The excited workers then zoom out of the hive to find their nearby treasure.

Food that is farther away from the hive is communicated by a **wagging dance.** First the bee runs in a straight line, wagging her abdomen. Then she runs in a half-circle, another straight line, and another half-circle, this time in the other direction. The completed dance forms a figure-eight pattern. The wagging dance tells the other bees at what angle to the sun the food source lies and how far away the food is. This dance is amazingly accurate, even if the food is miles away! The wagging dance is diagrammed in the photo on the right. Notice the other workers carefully watching the "dancer."

When there is no more room in the beehive—when all honeycomb cells are filled with brood, honey, or pollen—the majority of the colony prepares for **swarming,** or leaving the hive to find a new home. Swarming often happens in the spring and is accompanied by great excitement. First, worker bees start building peanut-shaped **queen cells** (below right) around some of the larvae already in the hive. They feed these larvae only royal jelly, and with this extra nutrition, they will emerge as queens in 16 days. Then a few bees, called **scout bees,** fly off to look for a new hive for the swarm.

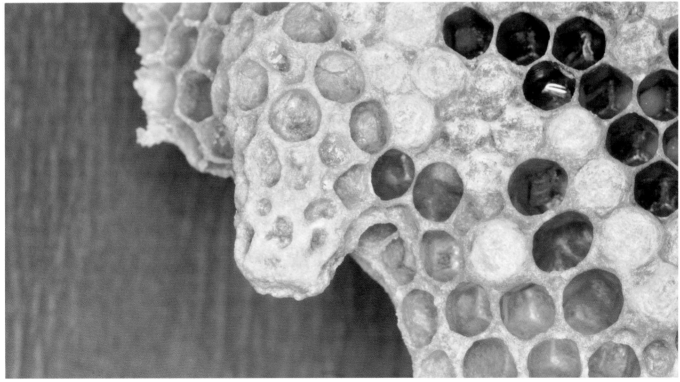

41

Knowing there will soon be a new queen, the old queen must leave, for there can be only one queen to a colony. Buzzing loudly, the bees clamber to the entrance of the hive. About half of the bee colony, including the queen, swarms out. No one knows what determines which bees will swarm and which will remain behind. The bees fly away, land on a tree, fencepost, or even a back-yard swing, and hang together in a cluster like a bunch of grapes. If at this point the swarm is not caught by a beekeeper, it follows the scout bees to its new hive in a hollow tree or other such place and lives as a wild swarm.

Back at the old hive, the new queen emerges from her cell. She immediately kills other young queens still in their cells so that she can rule the bee colony alone. The newborn queen has become the ruler of the bees that stayed behind when the others swarmed. Soon she goes on her mating flight, mates with one or more drones, and is ready to lay eggs. At this point the drones of the hive have fulfilled their life's work. They cannot help with any of the workers' chores. They are stung to death, driven away, or left to starve, because the workers can no longer spare precious food on these now-worthless members of the colony.

In cooler climates, workers that are still living when autumn comes form a wintering cluster and remain clustered until the next spring. By clustering, the bees keep each other warm. Because the beekeeper took much of the delicious, sweet honey from the hive in the summer and the bees are therefore short of food for the winter, the beekeeper feeds them with sugar syrup. When spring comes again, the bees will fly out of their winter homes and busily begin their work, repeating the fascinating cycle of life we have just seen.

Glossary

beeswax: a substance secreted by honeybees' wax glands. Beeswax is used by honeybees for building the comb and for capping brood cells; humans use it in candles, lipsticks, and other products.

brood cells: cells in the honeycomb that contain eggs, larvae, or pupae

crop: a sac, separate from the stomach, in which honeybees store honey. Also called **honey stomach.**

drone: a male honeybee, developed from an unfertilized egg

fertilization: the union of male and female reproductive cells that in flowers occurs as a result of pollination

larva: a bee in the second stage of development before reaching adulthood

metamorphosis: the series of changes that take place in a honeybee's development from egg to larva to pupa to adult

pollination: the transfer of pollen, containing male reproductive cells, to the female parts of a flower

pupa: a bee in the third stage of development before reaching adulthood

queen: a female bee capable of laying eggs and responsible for keeping order in the hive

regurgitation: the process by which a worker bee pours out the nectar she has gathered.

royal jelly: a highly nutritious substance secreted by worker bees and fed to developing larvae

skep: a dome-shaped basketlike hive

swarming: the movement of a group of honeybees from their hive to start a new colony

venom: the irritating substance secreted by bees through their stingers

worker: a female honeybee not capable of reproducing. Workers perform nearly all the duties of the hive.

ABOUT THE AUTHORS

Heiderose and Andreas Fischer-Nagel received degrees in biology from the University of Berlin. Their special interests include animal behavior, wildlife protection, and environmental control. The Fischer-Nagels have collaborated on several internationally successful science books for children. They attribute the success of their books to their "love of children and of our threatened environment" and believe that "children learning to respect nature today are tomorrow's protectors of nature."

The Fischer-Nagels live in Germany with their daughters, Tamarica and Cosmea Désirée.